A gift for:

My mom
Happy Mother's Day!
~~From:~~
Love,
Ave
2004

Thanks a Bunch, Mom!

ILLUSTRATED BY

BARB TOURTILLOTTE

J COUNTRYMAN

Joy...the simplest form

of gratitude.

—Karl Barth

Children are a work of heart.

They grow best with love.

—Anonymous

Thanks for giving me
room to grow.

"At whatever point Mother
touches life, she always brings
a lilt and a lift to it.
That's why I smile whenever
I think of her."

—Catherine Marshall

Thanks for the smiles
you brought to my life—

for the tears
you gently soothed away,

and for the sunshine
no one but you

could bring to a cloudy day.

Home is where your mother is.

Thanks for making our home
a place with a little perfection,
loads of playtime,
and plenty of praise.

All her gentle long life through

Mother is bent on nursing you;

And though you may be grown.

She still claims you for her own.

To her you will always be

Just a youngster at her knee.

—Edgar A. Guest

Thanks for always loving me
and for letting me know
I will always be
"the youngster at your knee."
Which, by the way,
is fine with me!

Mother's little practices of love:

 hot oatmeal on cold winter mornings

 lullabies

 goodnight prayers and kisses

 making time to have fun with me

 kisses and Bandaids where it hurts

A little rain can straighten a flower stem.

A little love can change a life.

—Max Lucado

Thanks for never holding me
at arm's length—
for always holding me
close in your love.

In all this world through all of time

There could not be another

Who could fulfill God's purpose

As completely as a mother!

—Helen Steiner Rice

It is certainly fair to say
there could never be
another mother
exactly the right fit for *me*.

A happy women is one
who has no cares at all;
a cheerful woman is one who has cares
but doesn't let them get her down.

—Beverly Sills

Thanks for living before me
the notion that giving up is impossible.

Mother instructed me
in cooking, baking,
cleaning, washing, ironing
and mending.
But most of all,
Mother taught me to love
the Lord and His Word.

—Eunice Will

Thanks Mom!
Though you had little time to spare,
you taught me how important it is
to make time for prayer.

And thanks for teaching me
that the smallest steps
can change your life.

THANKS FOR UNDERSTANDING
THE IMPORTANT THINGS:

There can never be too many
cookies in the cupboard.

There can never be too many chocolate
chips in a chocolate chip cookie.

Kids and noise are compatible.

It's okay to lay on the picnic table
and watch shooting stars.

 Dogs and kids can cuddle
on the couch.

 Love is shown best in little things.

 Every day needs space for surprises.

 A giggle is a good thing.

 A little dirt never hurt anybody.

Her children respect and bless her;

her husband joins in

with words of praise:

"Many women have done

wonderful things,

but you've outclassed them all!"

Proverbs 31:28–29 [The Message]

How I enjoy the simple pleasure
of just being together with you.
No matter what we do,
it's bound to be much more fun
than most of the things
I might have done
with anyone else but you.

Those who bring sunshine
into the lives of others
cannot keep it
from themselves.

—James M. Barrie

To have a loving mother

is one of the best

of God's good gifts.

—Anonymous

Thanks for telling me that
God is in every little thing;
that He guides the angels
and the sparrows, too;
that He molds a tear and
carves the Grand Canyon.

The mother is the most precious
possession of the nation.

—Ellen Key (1926)

Thanks for reminding me again
and again that we create
our tomorrows by what
we dream today.

As a mother comforts her child,

so I will comfort you.

Isaiah 66:13 (niv)

Thanks for making me feel safe,
secure, and cared for.

It's okay to let your children know
you are proud of them.
They thrive on your approval.

—Grace Ketterman, M. D.

Thanks for believing in me.

Thanks for letting me
make mistakes.

Thanks for trusting me.

THANKS FOR NOT ONLY TEACHING ME
BUT FOR SHOWING ME THAT:

People are like river stones.
The most beautiful are those
who have been tossed by the winds
and washed by the waters of life.

Being nice is not a sign of weakness,
it's a sign of courtesy.

If you don't paddle your own canoe
it won't move.

It's important to show respect
in little things—like putting
the cap back on the toothpaste.

One of the nicest things
you can give anybody
is kindness.

You can't help others
without helping yourself.

Thanks for encouraging me
to run to win even if
I didn't stand a chance.

A good laugh is sunshine in a house.

—William Thackeray

Thanks for insisting that if the birds can sing
after a storm so should we.

FLUTTering

chirping

BUZZing

Blooming

People who love each other
fully and truly are the happiest people
in the world. They may have little,
they may have nothing,
but they are happy people.

—Mother Teresa

A BOUQUET

VERBENA
faithful

PHLOX
warm feelings

VIOLET
hope

DOGWOOD
durability

LAVENDER
love and devotion

for MOTHER:

PINK
ROSES
grace and beauty

BLUE
BELL
constancy

LILAC
hope

HONEYSUCKLE
generous and devoted affection

That best portion of
a good [woman's] life,
[her] little, nameless,
unremembered
acts of kindness
and of love.

—William Wordsworth

A MOTHER IS:

A guaranteed lifetime supply of hugs.

The one who will sing with you
on the mountain and hold your hand
through the valley.

A great sounding board—
she'll give you feedback
whether you want it or not.

Always ready to give you her jacket on a cold day, her window seat in the tour bus, or her ticket to the Rose Bowl.

A little like God. She knows your faults but loves you anyway.

Good kids are like good soup.

The best are always homemade.

—Anonymous

Thanks for praising me
in public,
and disciplining me
in private.

Every house where love abides

and friendship is a guest,

is surely home, and home sweet home,

for there the heart can rest.

—Henry Van Dyke

Thanks for the gift
of goof-off days.

Reading a message from my mother,

I am a child again and a longing

unutterable fills my heart

for Mother's counsel,

for the safe haven

of her protection

and the relief

from responsibility.

—Laura Ingalls Wilder

GAZANIA
SEEDS

PETUNIA
BARB T.

ia
Snaps
Pansy

The Lord bless you

and keep you dear Mother.

Thanks a bunch!